Vigils of the Night Office

Poetry and Prose Poetry by Paul Edward Costa

Vigils of the Night Office

Copyright © 2025 by Paul Edward Costa

Front cover © by DarkWinter Designs

Front cover image © Paul Edward Costa

All rights reserved. No part of this book may be used for AI training purposes or reproduced in any form or by any electronic or mechanical means including information storage and retrieval systems, without permission in writing from the author. The only exception is by a reviewer, who may quote short excerpts in a review.

First Printing: February 2025

Published by **DarkWinter Press**: www.darkwinterlit.com

All rights reserved.

ISBN: 978-1-998441-21-1

For Shannon Christie, Cody Vaters, Skye Nutbean,
Chatherine Chhina, Dave Haskins, and John Ambury.
R.I.P.

Advance Praise for Vigils of the Night Office

"*Vigils of the Night Office* is a bold and imaginative journey woven together by vivid metaphors and incisive storytelling. Amid the dystopian undercurrents of Costa's Orwellian warnings, there is hope. This collection rewards careful attention, offering both intellectual rigour and artistic grace – more than a great work of fiction, *Vigils of the Night Office* is a wake-up call for humanity to be and do better."

Raymond Helkio, Director, Poet, Art Director, Artist, Teacher, and Host of the Poetry Open Mic at Buddies In Bad Times Theatre. Playwright of *Brick & Skipper and LEDUC: A Public Life of Solitude*.

"Paul Edward Costa is a dynamic presence on Toronto stages as a poet, emcee and community builder. In *Vigils of the Night Office*, he makes a leap from the stage to the page with his trademark passion and bristling energy."

Bruce Hunter, Poet and Author of *In the Bear's House*

"Paul Edward Costa's *Vigils of the Night Office* speaks to us through a dark sieve in an unflinching voice, both futuristic and current, layered with eerie incandescence. A work of profound imagination and deft poetic craft."

Clara Blackwood, Poet and Author of *Pomegranate Heart*

"Paul Edward Costa's *Vigils of the Night Office* pushes its reader into a place where convictions are meant to be questioned and emotions demand to be expressed. His written word manages to evoke an experience that echoes the way he performs; whether out loud or on a page, Costa's poetry will compel you to think and feel. This collection is not meant to be restful, but that is what is beautiful about it. Be prepared for a ride."

Valery Brosseau, Public Speaker, Mental Health Professional, Author, Poet, and Teacher. Brazilian Jiu-Jitsu Purple Belt.

"I've been thinking a lot of people who achieve big firsts, going where no one like them has before, and who instead of opening the way for others to follow, choose to pull the ladder up after them. Paul's "To Those Who Vandalise Ladders" speaks directly to the shame at the heart of that urgency, to make sure that no one follows your footsteps back to your lower origins. Like so many of his works, these eloquent little bites of philosophy and observation, these *Vigils of the Night Office* take me into worlds that I know and interactions that I fear or covet and twist their appearances to unfold greater meaning. Sometimes as I read, I feel I've fallen under the spell of an intellectual podcast that threatens to deliciously destabilise my more staid preconceptions; other times I find myself looking out through my own eyes at a familiar scene, sharing a shake of the head or a small smile with the poet."

Jen Frankel, Poet, Author, Storyteller, and Host/Organiser. Author of the novel *Undead Redhead* and the poetry collection *Mayhaps: Poetry of Longing, Loss & Love*.

Table of Contents

VIGIL I: PUSHED, FILED, STAMPED, INDEXED, BRIEFED, DEBRIEFED, OR NUMBERED (On Government and Bureaucracy) 1

HERD ROYALTY 2
CASUALTIES OF THE LIQUID NITROGEN WAR 3
TO THOSE WHO VANDALISE LADDERS 5
TAKING CANDY FROM THE INFERNAL MACHINE . 7
ALL IN THE STATUS QUO SQUARES 8
MOTHER OF EXILES, THE TORCH OF HOPE 9
VAINGLORIOUS PURPOSE! 11
LETTER OF LUCIFER TO THE GENOCIDERS 13
YOU CAN'T REFLECT HERE; THIS IS THE PRAYER ROOM 15
THERE'S WISDOM IN THE CRIMSON MURAL 17
REVISIONIST MORTICIANS FOR HIRE 19

VIGIL II: I HAVE SEEN THE FUTURE, BROTHER (Speculative Writing) 21

DEEP SPACE ZERO 22
MECHANICAL PATHOS THEORY 23
THE ULTRAVIOLET MITIGATOR 25
THE RAGEWORLD OF MR. THOMAS 26
ETHEREAL INK BLEEDING THROUGH 28
GRAVITATIONAL FIELD SYNDROME 29

LANDING ON PERPLEXIUM 9 31
VIGIL III: THE REALM OF REANIMATION (On Beings Brought Back to Life).. **33**
IN THE REALM OF REANIMATION 34
RETURN TO THE REALM OF REANIMATION 35
LESSONS FROM THE REALM OF REANIMATION ... 36
BATTLE FOR THE REALM OF REANIMATION 37
VIGIL IV: SURFING WITH AN ACID TONGUE (Caustic Commentary and Critique) **38**
TOO QUIET ON THE OPEN FRONT 39
ADVERTISING IN A CONFORMATIVE MARKETING ENVIRONMENT 40
THE WINDOW TRUMPET'S RECEDING TONES 41
THE BOOTLICKER'S BAR ROOM EPIPHANY 43
CONFESSOR FOR THE PROSECUTION 45
THREE STARS AND BURNT TOAST 47
FROM THE REAR-GUARD DEBATE CLUB 48
EVERYBODY WAS SHADOW CARRYING 49
ALL THE PRODIGAL PEOPLE (WHERE DO THEY ALL COME FROM?) 51
VIGIL V: FULL OF SCORPIONS IS MY MIND (On Mental Health) **54**
WALKING SHADOWLESS 55
FUNERAL FOR A PRIVATE HALLUCINATION 56
I CHOSE…POORLY 57
PHANTOM SHIP LIGHTHOUSE 59

THE BIZARRE BREAKROOM NEAR THE GARDEN OF EARTHLY DELIGHTS.................. 60

SILENT NIGHT OF THE SOUL 61

EFFEXOR WITHDRAWAL VARIATIONS 62

DOCTOR LOWLAND'S GREETING CARDS 64

VIGIL VI: PILLARS OF FAITH (On Spirituality, Religion, and Myth)... 66

DEACONS OF THE DEEP....................... 67

TALES FROM THE SECRET KEEPER........................... 68

THE ANGELS OF OUR SYNCHRONISED AWARENESS 70

VIGIL VII: THOSE POETS, THEY STUDIED RULES OF VERSE (On Poetry) 72

FORGED IN VERSE.................................. 73

ENTER THE LIQUID WORD................................ 75

A DIFFERENT TAKE ON JO JONES THROWING A CYMBAL AT CHARLIE PARKER......................... 76

VIGIL VIII: PRESSING FLOWERS INTO PERFUME (Involving Flora)... 78

IMPRISONED ON THE THRESHOLD 79

KNIFE DEMONS IN THE SHAPE OF GENTLEMEN 80

FUME IMMUNITY 81

ROSE OCEANIA.. 83

VIGIL IX: PROLONG THE EXPERIMENT (Longer and Experimental Poetry) 85

THE ROSE PETAL SWORD STYLE 86

EMOTIONAL ARMOUR MERCHANT..................... 92

THROUGH THE PATTERNS AND THE SOUL 95
STARING DOWN THE REDUCED BLUE DRAGON
AND THE MAN CLOTHED IN MOONS 97
ON THE DAY LOU REED DIED 100
About the Poet **106**

VIGIL I

PUSHED, FILED, STAMPED, INDEXED, BRIEFED, DEBRIEFED, OR NUMBERED

(On Government and Bureaucracy)

HERD ROYALTY

If they'd seen our present with more prescience,
past thinkers might have added
    that, in the future,
        everyone will be a ruler
        of fifteen square centimetres
with no overlord
    able to opiate amassed individuals
    seeing the cogs they are as crowns,
where dark cruelty
    lies in the millimetre wide border
    between single cell kingdoms
whose shallow depths
    make each point of contact
    a stark struggle for survival
    among spectators feeling that they're really
    speakers in waiting
without time to waste
    on what they reflexively call
    the extravagant act of listening.

CASUALTIES OF THE LIQUID NITROGEN WAR

We thought it safe
to start construction –
the concrete foundation
    seemed all set.

We didn't know
    how four-hour planning meetings
    with poker faces
        evaporated trust,
and that every department
had rushed ahead,
secretly building
   private places beneath the communal layout
   of given blueprints.

They made hidden
    subterranean halls
    and airtight headquarters
in honeycomb gaps
   under poured cement

so a lead architect hangs their head
   then goes quiet
   before staring blankly
        beyond the fourth wall,
when that conceived
     cross-disciplinary temple
     collapses through the thin cracker

of its base
>   with so many hollow cavities
>   below high promise,
every floor folding
  and falling into the one supporting it
in an updated House of Usher
    where the last family descendent
        has enough engineering knowledge
            to experience the extra tragedy
            of predicting cataclysms
            they still can't stop—
                        or even prevent.

TO THOSE WHO VANDALISE LADDERS

What part
of looking down ladders
disturbs you enough
to kick out rungs
after climbing them?

I don't believe it's a wish
   to not go back
  or some twitch
     set off by vertigo,
as much as fear of a view
depicting your formative
imperfect years,
the slips and strained grips
prideful climbers
wish they could erase
     from tales of their formulation,
elevating myths
about deserving to stand alone
               atop great cliffs,
resisting urges
to leap over
out of guilt after seeing
beaches filled with every body that fell

in the fog of distance,
enabling delusions
that the shore's dark spots

are only insects
on lower scales of evolution.

TAKING CANDY FROM THE INFERNAL MACHINE

The hell engine lives
    by convincing its fuel
    that all other paths
        except the one
        leading to its intake valve
    are invalid,
saying that they're
Nothing but evaporation fields
        without purpose,
certainly not
        open plains of ascension
        on which footprints remain,
            standing out
    long after you're absorbed
into rhythms of the earth.

The hell engine seduces its prey
            deceitfully,
passing off mania's
        frantic heat
as love's
    warming embrace,
pretending internal combustion's
        roaring entropy
is actually a defined evolution
        towards some perfect state.

ALL IN THE STATUS QUO SQUARES

By some
    situational irony,
    the concept of
    rigid organisation
    gets more glowing praise
    from chaotic beings
    exploiting the void
    between airtight public squares:
the agents of mayhem
saying 'staying is safety,
   and arrivals are evil',
  then send all else to garbage disposals
          beyond the peripheral
    near sanctuaries they've conditioned
    not to believe anything
    that finds ways
    of crawling back through;

    with clear perspectives
    on all orbiting cubes,
an escapee's mania is even more revolting
    for the crystalline logic of the ranting they do,
      slipping through our first line of
          dismissive filters
before balanced vision
    undermines their warnings
    about the forbidden knowledge found
    while spinning 'till dizzy
in a no-man's land
    surrounded by tragically imploding cities.

MOTHER OF EXILES, THE TORCH OF HOPE

After burning
three billion dollars
our government
finally built a being
    with abilities
        beyond scientific reasoning:

their successful subject
    gained strange, specific powers
      for transmuting any liquid bottles
          into Molotov cocktails,
an alchemist changing water
        into combustible fluids,
        all containers
        into breakable glass,
        all lids
        into burning wicks,
        and any kind of bottling plant
        into a warehouse,
        stockpiling
        lethally incendiary weapons.

Despite that
    their super soldier never saw activation
because administrative officials
    couldn't agree
    on a code name designation:

literalists wanted
        Captain Molotov,
educated diplomats
with extra erudition
        thought *General Midas*
was a better, more creative moniker
        for someone whose touch
            gave purified matter
                a practical military application

though, in the end,
    it wasn't semantics
    or a capacity
    for creating eternal, flaming agony
    that sparked the project's cancellation.
    It was worry
        over the implications
        of showing the world
           how to make heat lamps for free,
           turning water into petrol
           as valuable as what's sold
           by anyone's
                geopolitical rivals.

VAINGLORIOUS PURPOSE!

Truthfully, nobody understood
the Leader's darkly obscure logic
for accusing many of villainy
                and declaring all-out war.

Decay at the top brought clawing,
anarchic hate from a crop of voices whose distaste
made them feel full-stop separate
                and immune to a falling framework

while the largest legion supporting the Leader's ascension
was one in a region of thought
that advocated the benefit
                of tying bile ducts off

before releasing built-up poison
and turning speech into a song of enabling silence
when told to *Speak now*
                or prolong the rising conflict.

A usual wholesale uprooting of files
followed the ensuing war's end,
revealing their Leader's purpose
                for boiling the earth in tension:

He'd conjured a vision of the world's unavoidable demise
and made the decision to give war's supposed purpose
to people, less fearful of that evil
              than what happens when a mind awaits obliteration.

He chose that course while alone with the power in his head
and no one around who could force another view
that a person might endorse love as their last emotion instead
        by stopping to feel
           what life still remains in the queue.

LETTER OF LUCIFER TO THE GENOCIDERS

   I saw what you did there,
as I stood nearby, admiring
         your bold strategy:

one step back
and two ahead,

widen your range,
kill them all
      then resurrect
      only who's requested by popular demand
      according to supply chains you control.

Bodies with deviant dispositions
keep feeding worms

while your preferred traits
become paragons of virtue,

and this selection
seems like the will of the people
far beyond the authority
of one
prosecutable person.

There'll be no more attacks or crackdowns,
just a set of indefinitely delayed priorities.

Then resistance will be seen
as *An extreme exercise in vain futility,*

and the strongest calls to stand down
will come as expressions
        of care for one's safety.

        * * *

Today
you can't
hunt a target openly;
even excuses
   on official letterhead
   smear as if soaked in rain
      while bearing the weight
        of experienced history
where minds are getting wise
to the trajectory
of a hammer swung directly.

That's why the delicate art
    of a deceptive hammer-throw
      is important now
        for connecting their catching capabilities
          to the intent of what you hurl
          from behind a veil
        of *Only meaning well,*
and the sturdy defence in believing
      you alone aren't responsible
      for what they fail to receive.

YOU CAN'T REFLECT HERE; THIS IS THE PRAYER ROOM

We didn't renovate the war room
into a space
for serene contemplation
because we wanted a temple
          of charming irony.

We did it to make that place
over in the image
of its original purpose,
   as every war room
        with a long meeting table,
        an ominous map,
        and hushed voices
        grand declarations
started somewhere
as a desperate desire for an area
free from the constant anxiety of espionage
        and the trauma in an anonymous
              artillery barrage
that can, if careless, mutate into mirrored aggression
gradually matching
        the opposed oppression,
   an equal and opposite reaction
    rooted in a twisted attraction
to what we most despise,
and a preference for anger's illusion
of control, as well as pride,
over a perceived patheticism

in being aware enough
to negotiate
the encroaching
all-encompassing chasm.

THERE'S WISDOM IN THE CRIMSON MURAL

The most moving mural wasn't one I found far off
across a fantasy ocean, but one I passed often
before the day I saw it for real and stood still to see
drawn words I could then fathom, using aged ability,
without being thrown by thinking of texts targeting me.

Immediately the question is whether I've had a
solid culmination of evolution or only
an impulsive, fading reaction borne of frustration

so I head out across ice shelves and up blue flower slopes
to a mountain temple of altered personal essence.

All the scholars in that distant, mythic school try locating
a moment of instantaneous change lying in a
transitional period—a long-form gradual shift

until the sudden switch between lead-up and fallout hits.

They might help me understand my day of epiphany
more than all the king's counsellors and all the king's planners
who, rightly, say change is slow and most often dull

while omitting breakthroughs or watershed revelations
to manage expectations, normalising how often
problems have no solution, where no one is at fault,
and awful happenings have no particular reason

since causes galvanise, instants of emergence reveal
who was present with hands on red, freshly painted levers
and such luminous clarity cannot be allowed by
the same covert culprits contained in that pocket dimension.

Benches line the wall opposite the mural, but paid guards
chase away anyone absorbing its layout who looks
a bit too close to some new, glowing state of awareness
and confidence that won't bring them back in desperation
to read – for some direction – designed, updated phrases
curators insist were always there, unaltered, from the start.

REVISIONIST MORTICIANS FOR HIRE

Our premium service retrieves the bodies of fallen soldiers on battlefields before taking them all the way to an anointed graveyard of your choosing for honourable, lasting burial at an enduring memorial site whose inscription omits any mention of the recent war in which they fought.

However, should you find yourself short on funds, we offer more affordable, budget options for sparing your deceased loved one the indignity of looting by humans, feeding by ravenous animals, or the dishonourable debasement of natural decay. Many prefer this to leaving relatives in physical association with the recently concluded conflict: our rangers track their location and pull them to the nearest fortified hill or otherwise strategic high-ground position. Placing them there gives the impression to any future being uncovering their remains that they at least died defending something of logically understandable purpose.

A quarter of our premium price has us put your soldier's body over another one nearby in a selfless, protective sprawl provoking deep heart swells at the sight of such a strong human bond.

While not the same as a formally distinguished tombstone, if you view the bigger picture you'll understand the peace these actions can bring; scholars of future civilizations will commemorate your loved one for at least being one of the few who expired with some honour and decent purpose in a wider conflict they'll inevitably see as a senseless slaughter in service of imperial abstractions.

VIGIL II

I HAVE SEEN THE FUTURE, BROTHER

(Speculative Writing)

DEEP SPACE ZERO

Each one went on,
longing for explorations of infinite,
only to scorch nerves
      in pitch-black basements
         after power grids fail completely
and eyes scream
    to their systems
      that *We're voyaging back*
         into pre-conscious dreams.

MECHANICAL PATHOS THEORY

Evolution's next stage,
    may let intent move
           inanimate matter
              as much as mechanical law:

with gifts given out of obligation
        dissolving into dust,

and birthday candles not going out
in gusts from Aeolus' lungs.
      if those around
         are bound by icy fear
            more than united love;

parts needed
    for friendship and loyalty
will have worn out on entropy's
              steady march ahead,
            replaced instead
              by effectively applied leverage;

parties can become
        automaton conventions
             with set, windup sequences
                initiating an embrace
            and registration forms
              flesh-covered fingers
                will be too feeble to fill out.

On the flipside
of that endlessly rotating coin
it won't be clear
   when intent makes movement
or when motion occurs
     of its own volition.

Monument makers
may shrug and half-smile
         before great feats

            free standing by way of polished planning?

or just enough goodwill
to pay off gravity's gunmen,
      shooting down
        whoever defiantly
             reaches past its grasp.

In that era,
    air has the capacity
        to carry lovers' lamentations
as they come to realise
        how romantic displays
won't always preserve
        the frame of a house they never maintained.

THE ULTRAVIOLET MITIGATOR

This machine shows the defendant's perceived inner-reality:

He's in a cramped warehouse. White paint spreads over psychedelic walls.

He's looking at a photograph. It shows him on a terrace with hanging vines. The picture is authentic. He knows he stood there, but can't recall how that vegetation smelt in the spring air. He tries, but manifests nothing.

The doors are welded shut. A rotary phone rings and voices make futile attempts to articulate how the terrace feels. His tics become—and remain—unsustainably volatile, though he doesn't say stop for fear of losing their company.

Consider this insight during sentencing.

THE RAGEWORLD OF MR. THOMAS

It took so long for the planet to build back up to a place of possible progress and innovation. The last soldier of the final conflict's winning side—half-nude, mud-covered, and crazed—clubbed the last enemy soldier to death with an energy mace whose battery died long ago. They claimed victory for their cause and drew its flag with dirt as a medium on the one remaining building in the city. It only had three walls and no roof.

***

Our future selves, do not go on like this again.

"Mr. Thomas, call on all your power and focused research skills to isolate a specific time and place for our use." With that, they ordered their greatest mind to go forth and forge a malleable pocket dimension. The trap was that—once built—only Mr. Thomas himself could alter it, making him its forced steward.

And what kind of cut-off subworld did he develop after stroking his beard in ponderance? He found that what worked also disgusted him. He built a barren, dry dirt realm of existing annihilation first, since that's how the place would end up after opposing forces went there to fight out their battles, but wars in such an environment didn't satiate those addicted to their purposeful, final carnage. Mr. Thomas eventually had to use the purple, augmented magic he exuded to construct an exquisite infrastructure there after each conflict—and before the next—with architecture complex enough to grant satisfaction in its collapse.

ETHEREAL INK BLEEDING THROUGH

There was a time when Star Barons sewed subtle writing
through heavens high above any earth-bound heads.
That was enough, in an era that eventually ebbed
into new sets of nebulous notations
that needed to be
spelt out plainly in searing starlight.
But still, people down there didn't alter their demeanour.
And when priests of space passed through a purple dusk
in gear of grey robes below gyroscope wreaths,
they looked all around
and found how humans had
       deleted their sight
        in an act of blind fear,
       or of what they felt
          was their only remaining
          way of resisting
             an incalculably vast
               egotistical will.

GRAVITATIONAL FIELD SYNDROME

     A unique phenomenon of the alien invasion was how their low-flying attack ships affected denizens of the areas through which they passed while decimating our infrastructure, our humming communication hubs, and our glowing temples of power,
    an inversion of expected effect,
        the blatant disconnect
    when unleashed fire-winds and matter-melting
                sapphire beams
    perversely drew human prey
   to their saucers by self-directed means:
   diving from helicopters or planes, jumping off high towers, or hooking to them like fish angling for boats, there came people determined to climb on though they never got aboard.
    Was it all
     for the thrill
     of surfing alien discs
     or using tethers to be like tendrils?
     Did they abruptly leap into abduction?
    No—those weren't the motivations they had uploaded online before setting out...
 and eventually losing their grip, slipping off, asphyxiating, or freezing as they aimed recordings towards the extra-terrestrial consciousness exclusively (who may have never heard it) while we grabbed the signal.
    Simple, cynical
     announced defections

      to the winning side
           didn't come through the static.
  What followed were passionate proclamations of utility and heritage, the people swearing they always had been officers of the spacefaring race or that they were actual biomechanical augmentations to the ships, serving the function of antenna, scanners, or weapons (should they hold a firearm with which they could shoot the Earth).
    Some attempted alien speech
    but not one of them articulated
        the same phonetics as any other;
    some survived the fall back to earth and dove into equally impassioned declarations of having never sworn their functioning as star-borne technology or their possession of off-world DNA.
    Their close proximity
  physical contact with the invading force
  fuelled the fever
  of inconclusive investigations
    and the sheer whiplash of such extreme reversals left Earthlings not affected almost as a different species entirely, questioning how a syndrome like this could exist…
    Or was disrupted self-knowledge
  and division
    the effect of an attack method
            beyond our perception?
  Because everyone doubting
  what to believe about themselves
    or anyone else
        found little around which to unite in the end.

LANDING ON PERPLEXIUM
9

Oval discs opening
for uncoiling cables,
single tentacles slipping
  between disembodied lips

set fixed
       in *out there's*
       dull ochre dusk,

Spherical helmet
        headlamp lights
        roam amid descents
        to a promenade
outside palace gates,

invisible signals combing
        a frozen tableau,
and readings whining on instruments
       whose science must be
       seventy years ahead of its time.

A gargantuan mainframe of information is gained

though they still cannot glean
the reason why a legion of petrified beings
        bow on one knee
        before the front wall

in everlasting respect
    for a structure cut into crystal cliffs,
or stand frozen
in an apocalyptic instant that hit
while desperate pilgrims
      knelt in fatigued frustration,
      shut out after following
        so long a crossing to that end,

carefully positioned,
torturously close to having viewed
      their desired destination.

VIGIL III

THE REALM OF REANIMATION

(On Beings Brought Back to Life)

IN THE REALM OF REANIMATION

    The realm of reanimation
touches reassembled monsters
    and stuffed animals
        sewn back together
        with sparks of violent fury.

But teddy bears and their kin
twist rusted garden tools
    into a victim's flesh
        with more malice
    than monstrosities
        who remember what it was like
        when they were hunted down,

        who aren't haunted
            by torturous memories
of lives
once warmed
    by adoration.

RETURN TO THE REALM OF REANIMATION

Animated toys,
destroyed and restored,
are the only items on our list
awaking with sadistic souls:
a line of dead objects shaking their fists,

a drawn-back bowstring,
retreating in timidity,
needing space. How can you say it hopes for a death?

It's the million mild concessions
cutesy charm demands.
Daily indignations return rising dividends.

Coveting stillness to block their way,
the highest spite grows as they pray,
and soft paws feel justified in channelling doomsday.

Don't you understand?
Did you endure a thousand backhands?
No? Well, *entrails for eyes* is now the law of the land,

where passive bunnies in soft pastel clothes
barely see what an honestly raw being knows,
that any flaw obscured from a private mirror still shows
when viewed by the eyes of public souls.

LESSONS FROM THE REALM OF REANIMATION

Leave it for linguists
        to figure out
        if summoning a ghost
        is the same
        as raising a corpse.

That conjuring's key step
doesn't require skilled incantations
as much as standing in a graveyard
        while simply insisting
that you'll pursue
plans on which the dead didn't follow through
before spiritual egos
orbiting corporeal forms
do what they do best
by rising to great heights
        purely out of spite,
            but also into
                cloud cover, concealing
                a clear, fulfilling view
of how much growth they've really gone through.

BATTLE FOR THE REALM OF REANIMATION

Here the danger
    isn't supernatural strength
powering corpses
coming to life;

it's forgetting
that you're fighting for survival
against zombies who have already faced
        game-over endings
        and, in extreme cases,
        the kill screen where a whole console's
        dream depletes,
who don't mind dislocating limbs
if they get to claim the resulting win

but in this nihilistic nightmare
even Viking warriors avoid the undead
and prefer their own divine balance
        of battles and banquets
to blighted peat bogs
where fresh bodies are so scarce
that our living dead
now prey on the compatriots
    who show the least amount of decay.

VIGIL IV

SURFING WITH AN ACID TONGUE

(Caustic Commentary and Critique)

TOO QUIET ON THE OPEN FRONT

That traveller
    encounters their contemplations alone
    beyond the convent's borders;
their nomadic road
    unspools from never knowing
    whether peace is earnest
  or only a case
    of someone taking years
    to charge an atom-shredding attack,
            meeting morality
              with total apathy.

Is it birds chirping in spring
      or a ticking countdown
        to cooling heat death
          coming around?

ADVERTISING IN A CONFORMATIVE MARKETING ENVIRONMENT

Maybe they're rebuilt with it.

Maybe it's naturally induced
empathy-affecting Botox
enshrining the muscles
        behind facial expressions
in affable,
deferential,
socially acceptable casts of politeness:
replicant facades,
tasteless and out of place,
like hiking near campsites
        in a Jason Voorhees mask

or standing motionless in the aftermath of a battle
                amid frantic medical personnel
while singing a sweet,
    perfunctory tune,
    doing nothing
    but shooting pure,
        uncut caramel's
        cloying tones
        towards severed cochlear nerves
        in aerated melodies
          that will never be heard.

THE WINDOW TRUMPET'S RECEDING TONES

I didn't ask
sound engineers exactly why
         my window, cranked open,
         amplified distant sounds
         from the direction of where it went ajar.
I had a vague idea
  but liked imagining
  that my window frame was a doorway instead
  to the wisdom collected by unfettered winds
gathering crisp spring air
         and fall's sweet decay
as well as my neighbour's operatic vitriol,
performed in a voice so used to contention
      that the early stage of an escalating argument,
      was its normal speaking tone,
        its permanently set volume,
a classically trained projection
      for his theatre of the driveway,
always one half of a phone conversation
      as if he were Peter Sellers
         as Dr. Strangelove's president,
     Bob Newhart's deadpan half of a pretend call,
or a commedia dell'arte version
of high theatre's family agitation.

I heard how *Fucking stupid*
      that fucking guy is
      so many times.

I confess that I may have
>	on one or two occasions,
>	escaped being deceived
>	thanks to the scepticism
>	his ramblings reinforced,
and that maybe,
here or there,
I found it inspiring to hear a gaunt, skeletal man
>	declare so confidently
>	that *I'm not afraid of anyone!*
>	after another argument outdoors
in a stiff breeze that might blow him over,
>	while carrying on
>	the bare seed of that determination
>	to germinate in whoever
>	>	turns their ears towards the white noise of the wind.

THE BOOTLICKER'S BAR ROOM EPIPHANY

I fell into the trap
of taking surface-level fictions
at face value
before overhearing
a bar room conversation
that restored the angles of my better vision:

two dining companions –
one, with compassion and a heartfelt tone
    lamented an acquaintance's
    loss of friends,
    their sudden isolation
        from a social circle,
        and the sadness around that situation.

The other paused,
        wiped their mouth before a sip of beer
    and asked, *Is this the same person*
        who performed pantomime impressions
        mocking those close to them
        behind their backs
        in moments of crisis?

    So reminded,
    the first diner confessed,
    that *Yes, yes, they did,*

as the special silence

      of a broken spell came down

while the second one's serrated knife
         dissected their undercooked steak
    with a sharp, goosebump-raising squeak
           coming off the ornate plate.

CONFESSOR FOR THE PROSECUTION

Witness testimony
got so confusingly
    contradictory,
the truth had to be
that those accused
either mastered misinformation,
the art of coordinating deception,
or were so thoroughly incompetent
their destructive actions
came from strokes of corrupted luck,
        hideous intent created,
with more malicious potential energy
        than real capability,

though that made little difference
in the objective suffering of all affected,
   the ones we disrespected as well

   by spinning a narrative
     of the defendants'
        Machiavellian machinations
without certainty,
so interest stayed alive
while public ideals
    met slowly turning judicial wheels

and to avoid seeing how a group
less than the sum of its facade

could shake our great institutions,
whose foundations
have malleable faith
    mixed into their cement.

THREE STARS AND BURNT TOAST

It's the worst version of frustration
when communication's self-professed masters
assume a preschool journal's
    vague, ambiguous style—
enough to make even the most patient,
                     meditative monk
lose their composure
and embark on our age's
        most violent massacre.

It's as if you bought a Caprice Classic
just to find the body beneath half-rusted
while your salesperson later
simply shrugs, as if they didn't
just express complete confidence that it would win
the twenty-four-hour endurance race of Le Mans.

Then you can only conclude,
as has been said other places,
        other ways,
that some journey so far eastwards,
with such singularly self-assured purpose,
they stay permanently grounded on a western shore.

FROM THE REAR-GUARD DEBATE CLUB

There's an oddity
in seeing debate clubs
four thousand miles from the front
use rapid fire voices
while fiddling
with ideas of violence

until I strained past a last post of emotion
and said: be it resolved
that minds steeped in abstract debates
about bloodstained issues
and the stark necessities of survival
should only enter a material plane
by printing their erudite input,
folding it four ways,
and sliding that stiff, thin edge asswards
to serve as a fractional reminder
of the discomfort dealt with
by lives lacking the privilege to pull back
and be brave from way out of range.

EVERYBODY WAS SHADOW CARRYING

Folly
thy name is thinking
        binding resolutions
might move a raging chimpanzee
            towards mercy,

      expecting
         you'll retain faculties for debate
in a tug-of-limbs contest,
   demanding full focus
         for every critical joule of force
         on which you call.

I wish
    bears made two rows
        and bowed as one,
        carried the conservationist
who got too close
        towards a site for burial
        under stones
        where grizzlies stood in a wide circle,
                swaying to and fro,
I do,
but what's true
is their carving him down
to a ribcage
and one
   undigested arm

    whose ticking watch
does not disturb the guilty beast
    who likely thought,
        ranger rifles were long hives
        for very aggressive bees.

Dipping from the upper world
        to one below
in search of a goal
is great
    except for higher plane points of view
bending over lower heaths
    until victories seen beneath
no longer resemble
        the wishes envisioned
        in surface temples.

Shadows cannot drink
    from underground rivers
        their bodies desired
    and towards which they dug,
as flesh never senses
a return to celestial vibrations
    at the arrival of nightfall
    like its shadow does
earlier and earlier
while moving through the heavens
        above autumn halls.

ALL THE PRODIGAL PEOPLE (WHERE DO THEY ALL COME FROM?)

Teaching high school
crosses into the realm of watching
a discovery channel
animal show;
fellow students
follow classmates with French fry containers,
like fish chasing shakers of food flakes
      across their aquarium's length.

I don't hear kind words anymore
I hear preludes
      to requested favours getting closer.

That's why I wait,
or wince,
at the first sign of even authentic compliments,
where fake remarks imitate reality so well
I can't escape suspecting any decent display
of only being made
from masterfully painted
paper mâché.

Getting my licence to drive
became more akin
to some occult seance
with old, departed voices suddenly phoning

in feigned friendship out of nowhere
           for rides to wherever
dressing up functional desire
as a genuine expression of care.

If we're going to fight,
I'd rather enter a feud with integrity.
Hate me, declare me your enemy,
let distaste fuel your creativity—
let's start an Apollo Creed-Rocky rivalry, almost friendly.
I've heard your opponents define you
and I'll accept those parameters
as long as I know where they are,
but holding out one hand
while extending the other's middle finger
makes me doubt the glitching ground on which I stand.

Do I, in my best Danny Devito,
scream *Ha! So you come crawling back?*
when the company that cut me off from a dream
deems my unpleasant heat just what they need
to thaw their nightmare's
frozen centre?

I'd like that but luckily
a lack of faith in self-stability
lifts my trust in an outside
angel of better nature
urging a bigger person
    to emerge from within me.

Sometimes it seems

that the narrow,
>   relative difference
between being compassionate
and laying down as a doormat
lies only in your perspective
>   on what sacrifice is.

VIGIL V

FULL OF SCORPIONS IS MY MIND

(On Mental Health)

WALKING SHADOWLESS

Youth is focusing
      on avoiding
      eventual isolation
      in sealed chambers
      erasing
      sensory perception.

Maturity is accepting
      how inevitably
      we head towards our solitude
      while wondering
      what wallpaper
          we'll paste over the abyss
as we utter our only wish,
      praying hopefully
      that relatively few wraiths
      follow our road to a confined infinite,
              filled with shifting mist.

FUNERAL FOR A PRIVATE HALLUCINATION

Few things feel so isolating
as mourning the loss of a space
   only I remember existing,
  alone among everyone unaware
  of the hidden sanctuary
     that once offered such care.

I might need a fellowship
of mental health professionals
excavating neurological doom
if I want healing

after viewing another world
between light's visible spectrum,
internalising its inner workings,
      its inherent spirit,
and living to tell
of the Ragnarök that engulfed it
in a remaining reality made up mostly
of the majority seeing light frequencies normally
who find my rarely told tale
of ultraviolet loss
     too abstract and exotic
to feel with any level of relatability;

they never knew its topic well enough
to weep as I did
while time and tragedy wiped that place away.

I CHOSE...POORLY

It's true,
   I can't pour from an empty cup

but I can melt it
into bits I chew
   for the illusion of digestion
   that lets someone function
       one more minute,
or down to a liquid,
   in the cast iron
       catch basin I tilt,
pouring that viscous substance
on whatever has lost
its natural shell

before scraping up plastic
from where it's set
or been spat out

just to start again,
with the cup I hold
   becoming a symbol
   more impressive and eternal
than my ever more
   malnourished
pedestal of a physical frame,

as observers
with too-distant

      utilitarian attitudes
ask why more things
aren't like
those nice stoic cups
you can usefully recycle,
or the unassuming one
that caught the blood of Christ
            without complaint.

PHANTOM SHIP LIGHTHOUSE

I mastered making melodies
           on a kazoo
      and still descended
       into the darkest depths of madness
for comparing my tone's
          material yield
               to that of Paganini's
                   elegant violin virtuosity,

    because I coveted
    the energy washing over idols
       more than the aura of figures
          emitting compatible frequencies
             wherever they may be:

            in shrouded highlands
            past remote highways
or somewhere between
ancient libraries
     filled with
        emotionally emaciated people
desperately seeking,
           but never finding,
tomes whose words
      are an explanatory transcription
         of the unusual wavelengths
            we walk on in isolation.

THE BIZARRE BREAKROOM NEAR THE GARDEN OF EARTHLY DELIGHTS

Slouching on a park bench,
smoking in suit and tie,
there's a Mennonite family
    riding the swings,
  and their horse-drawn carriage off to the side
    of a mill refitted
      for formal events.

Arriving texts
    ask if I'm alright:

They're serving dessert
  and the speeches start soon.

SILENT NIGHT OF THE SOUL

You've heard
about dark nights of the soul;
now prepare
for a soul's silent night:

basically the same,
but over year-end holidays
where slowing for celebrations
also lets baggage cars
      carrying twelve months'
      exclusions, extortions,
      and bitter losses,
compress against the front engine

enough to get baked on
as a crust you can soften
then chip off

or maybe, instead,
let burn into the oblivion
      of never again,

while swinging tools
in service of new roads
unhooked from a toxic locomotive's
      subhuman ghosts
      and decrepit codes.

EFFEXOR WITHDRAWAL VARIATIONS

A seasick clarity
washes over me
when I, for a moment,
hear musical movements made
by the percussionist on the other side of it all,
      but somehow still nearby,
when he shakes
my faith's skeletal remains
like a rainstick design upending cause and effect,
dropping dry thorns through me
as leverage moves minds
and emotions try moving
Newgrange into alignment
with new constellations.
Then, a brain-based electric sensation.
It's the chess piece realising their war
is one of solitary opposition
to the two kaleidoscopic colossi above them
as their compatriots are too attached
to the thrilling satisfaction
of being lifted through the air before landing
and displacing
the fellow being they see in their way
through a worldview
in the easily digestible
binary code of only two dimensions
Now the woozy quality of caffeine withdrawal.

So let me be a type
who accepts their flaws and acknowledges unpleasant
tendencies inside,
enough to adjust those habits,
or at least harness them to a purpose
so that I won't spend each moment spewing speech
at top volume,
drowning out
the strident, feedback-formed entity I've become,
like all unfortunate enough to be within earshot do
if I dance on flower beds,
asserting my right to pleasant aromas
while holding a butterfly in cupped hands
one twitch away from being crushed,
so no one dares interrupt
my inert flow of motion,
all to let me dream the lie of being
someone nurturing life without ego,
discharging perfume from each pore,
whose music—frequently requested—
              is always in rotation.
As these head-swimming hand tremors at the heart of irritation
come down

DOCTOR LOWLAND'S GREETING CARDS

Like dice having to land
        on one side in the end,
Dr. Lowland's deep psychiatric practice
became best known
for the greeting cards she gave patients,
at first glance
almost indistinguishable from available brands,
       except in how she signed off:

Her inscriptions held well wishes
             for weddings,
              new life arriving,
             a retirement,
             or whomever's birthday,
then helped free recipients
       from the pressures of positive thinking
        those cavernous, premade constructs demand
by opening a door
   refreshingly exposing
   the dark currents in sewers
   below every celebration,
as she put her signature
       not after *from*,
          sincerely, or *regards*,
but the plain, abrupt statement: *Tough shit*.

A toast to your new bond
with another life through love.

Tough shit,

Everything we do
moulds our next generation's world.
                      Tough shit,

You can finally have some peace and quiet
at home in your golden years.
                            Tough shit,

Just writing to honour you
completing another cycle around the sun.
                              Tough shit,

                    followed by her name
                    scrawled in a script,
                    shaky at first
                    but smoother
          after moving through the patterns
                            of written words.

VIGIL VI

PILLARS OF FAITH

(On Spirituality, Religion, and Myth)

DEACONS OF THE DEEP

Our debate's sound waves
broke over each other while birthing
                  this dark cathedral.
One demanding
   masochistic piety,
while unable to permit
        passive standing by pews
studded with splinters
and used syringes in areas
        for kneeling parishioners.

Say *Alright, point taken.*
If you really want to awaken the kraken:
since these sermons can't be heard,
              they have to be tattooed
on your skin's most sensitive surface
or else the walls will say
       You still haven't properly prayed,
       so, of course any lack of faith is your fault.

Electric egos don't react well
when I ground my voice against their current tantrum,
as pillars shift about the interior,
pressing together to pinch
whoever doesn't resemble penitent sculptures
                out of existence,
where, even after surrendering to that crushing pressure,
the mere resistance put up by a physical frame
will make the cathedral label you as its aggressor.

TALES FROM THE SECRET KEEPER

Turning charnel doors transparent
might show their contents
with more authentic clarity,
though that brings sacred cemetery sites
     closer to a zoo's exhibition rites.

Graveyard holding units
     house hoarded knowledge I can't forget
     or let infect friends' reflections
lest their faces shrink three sizes
     with taut expressions,
less able to show true emotions.

Tombstones and their plots crumble when Grave keepers
take pictures with visitors by the front gates
for fame from how nobly they hold dark hate
     in a place with a known location.

I'm the one walking back rows, orchestrating
trimmed lots, dignified markers
and enough opacity to not re-traumatize visitors
with a full view of what's decomposing,

but there's a second half-light cemetery
behind the eyes of crypt-keepers and mortuary staff:
    a night gallery's
      photographic pathology.

Remembrance is an afterlife through which walk the dead,
        as well as a fever oppressing the brain.
Drop an anchor too far into that void
     and the void sinks its hooks into you
while denying how this is normalises
     zombies as the garden gnomes of our generation.

Some amount of telekinesis
has to be set aside for keeping our thought viruses at bay,
       some fraction of withheld mental energy
       drilling holes in the public masks of those
       keeping vigil over image demons they've seen,
               even accidentally,
       leaving them all thought *A little off* by the locals
and right for this role in which they excel,
    not allowing rotten gas to escape
           into nostrils
           then onto souls
and in so doing, honouring the entombed
without sensationalising
       the tangled truth of their doom.

THE ANGELS OF OUR SYNCHRONISED AWARENESS

Re-formed angels, who recall
        crawling out of hell
and up purgatory mountain for atonement,
won't respond irritably
when asked to show their absence of flames.
It's the restored Nephilim, denying
        how many eyes they have,
who revert to Old Testament identities
whenever their love for the beautiful conceptions
the world now has of them
        in kids' Bibles and stained-glass designs
is questioned.
Mastering duality isn't the same
   as having a two-faced demeanour;
   conversely,
it shows an honest acceptance of nature,
   too raw for delicate retinas,
   those
antennae picking up the frequency
   of emotional soul content,
   selecting
what they see and then believe,
   more for survival than a desire to be cruel.

I say
give me someone who prays
        after slaying a selected target
because I don't believe

          that act is one of indulgence,
          buying a ticket out of hell:
I think it's one professing comfort
             with how we are the sparks
             of opposing forces grinding together
in the energy centre
some cultures call the heart.
I've disengaged
      from spinning linguistic sorcerers
      arbitrarily killing calves they waste
      under the guise
      of following heartfelt impulses
      leading away from past mistakes,
insisting that giving into corruption
      is a justified correction,
hacking out language algebra
and manipulating variables
      we thought stable
rather than acknowledge
      and learn from
forgone innovations
so every five years
we celebrate some
forgotten knowledge
each time it's rediscovered,
and execute geometricians
      protesting the motion to
      create a new term whose
      definition means *circle*
      as well as *straight line*
until both concepts
      seem basically interchangeable.

VIGIL VII

THOSE POETS, THEY STUDIED RULES OF VERSE

(On Poetry)

FORGED IN VERSE

Hear, O Smith of the heavens, what the poet asks:
How does your hammer continue its ringing
when no cult carves your name or icon on earth?
I inquire because I think you'll listen
          and understand
            for we're alike in the ways that
            you do real smelting, forging, and welding,
          in greatest risen heat,
          to craft the fabulous impressions
          for which all heaven takes credit,
                on white clouds, drifting far
from your sky forge
while we stitch together perceptive words
      in whatever coherent arrangements we can
to articulate what's felt
      but rarely described:
to make the spoken prayers
      that console or inspire
          both non-believers and the faithful,
to decorate atmospheres for ten thousand
        funerals, nuptials, and dedications,
but still be seen as so niche a discipline
that our incoherence is presumed
and our underground state is considered
   all part of the plan.
Then comes the answer
   in steel, morse code strikes
      from an unseen hammer:
The vital distinction

                isn't between what's human and what's godly
                    but between sentient beings
        maintaining shadow-soaked foundations
        and those collecting glorious light atop them
                        on both sides of equal necessity
                as easy smiles gathering
                            goodwill
                stave off attacks more
                            efficiently
        than highly respectable engineering—
        still critical
        in maintaining surfaces
        that get to glitter,
            giving them the inner light they use
            to entice the world.

ENTER THE LIQUID WORD

If *hurt business*
is a label for boxing,
  emotional hurt business
is my term
for crafting poetics
out of inner experience,
    throwing clenched words,
        carefully wrapped to last,
        against opposing wills,
like when a professional fighter's performance
  on press conference microphones
  or in calling out opponents
        post-victory
        alters all career prospects,
or when a good mastery
    of literary arts
    is the difference between
the direct, telegraphed aversion
in yelling *Your opinion means less than dirt!*
and the deceptive proximity
of a punch from one inch
by politely saying, instead,
that *Your entirely untenable preference is noted.*

A DIFFERENT TAKE ON JO JONES THROWING A CYMBAL AT CHARLIE PARKER

Today I read poetry
at the Kansas City Reno Club
because it's said
if you, for a second,
perform with anything less
        than an earnest attempt
        to fully activate your abilities
        at whatever level they may be,
without regarding
        time an observer might have spent another way,
        attention they can only give so much of in life,
 or their wealth,
then you see a brief, flashing vision
revealing drummer Jo Jones' ghost
just before
        a copper cymbal crashes at your feet, translucent
        and ringing out, while wobbling with fading energy
until it comes to a stop,
silently symbolising
        not frustration coagulated from condemnation,
as is often told,
        but the encouragement
            of extended afterlife insight
            into extreme, untapped potential

                        belonging to whoever it is he's haunting,
or mentoring,
as it's known after turning
to face the wraiths chasing you down.

VIGIL VIII

PRESSING FLOWERS INTO PERFUME

(Involving Flora)

IMPRISONED ON THE THRESHOLD

You're warning children
about floating
     floral toxins,
and yes, I admit
       demanding thoroughness
for youthful wellness
   should always be standard,
but iron links
between flowers and fatal venom,
reinforced too far,
freeze toddlers in deep fear
          before dandelion fields,
lost among thoughts
      depicting fatal chain reactions
should they disturb those spores
          of poisonous pollen.

KNIFE DEMONS IN THE SHAPE OF GENTLEMEN

Fairies as firefly lights,
a first emergence
   out of parkland plant life.

      City workers
         let the leaves grow over
their last mechanised manicure.

That glittering on a breeze going
      towards these charming predators,
      studying dismemberment
      as its own discipline,
      calling it an unsung artform
for which they
have never been acknowledged,
or so they often say,

demons nailing down
sympathetic stories
for undercover sorties
   into the human world
with the sole purpose of pinning
fairies to trees,
driving butterfly knives through wings
only visible when pierced by caterpillars
       who cracked their cocoons
         as newly formed metal blades,
           colder than the moon.

FUME IMMUNITY

The atmosphere can't decide if it wants to gallop
then soar,
or settle into exploring
           every galaxy within itself.
Poison left behind
these post-antidote scars,
looking so much like squiggles
scribbled by children,
free from the knowledge of how elements like
that exist,
               are made,
                or why.
Even a jazz band
at an art gallery opening
won't flush emerald gases
      from each toxic element
      we kept for convenient use,
where raindrops are jealous
of divine circles hovering
            halfway
between heaven and earth
eternally keeping a sacred
        geometric shape,
the one,
the zero
they'll only achieve briefly
in an act
that demands

a full expenditure of themselves
humbly colliding with
and accepting the reality of forces
    greater than they are,
    worn down by nothing
    but resurrection and persistence,
where we won't be the version of ourselves
    that eventually prevails.

ROSE OCEANIA

Only recently did my imagination
again take the shape of formations
revealing the rose
at the centre
of our radioactive research emporium's end:
its malfunctioning microwaves,
its cracked radium watches,
and dental x-ray arms gone rogue
as every technician melted
and the rose at the centre of one last study
blossomed abnormally,
its stem's aggressive green thorns unable
               to shred sharpened petals
                       multiplying perpetually.

Tunnels and halls in the valley complex
flooded with blooming rose heads,
small enough to fill your lungs
or large enough to smother a life

At last the mutating flower broke
off into subsections,
growing on to form the vast rose ocean
               this valley became,

over which helicopters take tourists
      on guided flights
           playing *Kiss from a Rose* through their headsets
and never mentioning the origins

of the phenomenon below,
preserving an economy
      based only on that
and charging foreign countries
to dump what they don't want
in razor-sharp,
    rose petal waves
        camouflaging any appearance of blood.

VIGIL IX

PROLONG THE EXPERIMENT

(Longer and Experimental Poetry)

THE ROSE PETAL SWORD STYLE

The depths to which
    one must sink to scale its heights
    is the step
    so many seeking to master this sword style
    can't move past.
Perfect,
professional,
preservation of accumulated knowledge won't help.
In fact,
it's those diamond minds,
    cut from birth
    and polished during
    every facet of their maturation,
who suffer the deepest,
    most searingly clear burning
    after failing to master
        this unusual method
        of weapon wielding,
since you need real indifference
    and the stillness of undeniable depression
    to plunge your fine sword
        through disrepair,
        naturally cooling the blade
        in a true lack of care
        and shattering it to pieces.
Only then
can a user
wield the hilt as a

wand to command broken,
disparate shards according
to their will.

Destroying it
solely for the purpose of gaining this ability won't work;
something
must temper your thoughts in apathy
for a time,
before withdrawing them at the right moment
to find a ruined,
uncared-for sword.

Then,
the rise
of binary
bias, as people
tend to cause
in the two general ways the technique was trained:
one fully exploring far-ranging formations possible
and one still in the mindset of swinging
a single, solid blade while fighting.
The latter, tied to traditional principles,
kept shards arranged in the shape of old sheaths
as if the floating bits were still one full, firm piece,
    either
    curved like a scimitar
    or straighter
    like a cutlass, or Zweihander.
The most effective
practitioners, the former, saw
how past old practices didn't

do well with their demands in
the first place—
  or mastered aged methods so well they
   saw the disadvantages marring them:
        only striking once,
following
 a linear path through space.

New masters held
less-heavy sword hilts
alone like wands as a
storm of localised
blade fragments
floated, as if magnetised, around them.

They could,
under the control of a learned wielder,
        all aim together at one goal,
        shredding an enemy, for instance,
        or confusing them
        in a seamless symphony of purpose
or they,
manipulated by the most masterful and aware,
might gather, disperse, spin, out, converge,
and meet the mass of those controlled by an opponent.

Steel shards
clashing together
one-on-one in heavy clouds
trying to vanquish their opponent's master
    everywhere in front, behind,
    above, and around, two foes

dancing with sword hilts far apart
through control manoeuvres,
in the eyes of the deadly sharp storms
they summoned to action
by splitting their forged brains
like the organist who conjures
one churned pattern of air
into deep, rhythmic rumblings,
with one hand so engaged
while the other teases sharp notes
of treble melodies
into completely different
musical arrangements,
a state that's only
attainable through lengthy
practice where dull,
drilled repetition gives way
to internalisation.

That's when you stop trying hard
to let go and then
really do,
like letting your line-of-sight un-focus as you sense
                                       periphery details,
possible after purging
oneself of the urge
to then feel
like you must lock on and look directly at something
                                                         to behold it,
a constructed condition, falsely connecting
the concepts
of appreciation

and obsession.

The current frontier of research in this discipline studies how
                     to control sword fragments in such
                     advanced decay after cracking apart that
                     they, through age or repeated use,
                           crumble into morsels of metallic dust.

We used to think that shattered blades of the Rose Petal style
grew useless after wearing out, but the exact opposite of that
                                 became the case:
steel swords dissolved into dust and tiny slivers that could
                     still be controlled then brought
                     back together as one blade or
                     expanded into a misty, silver cloud
                     capable of
                               entering an opponent's pores or
                               airways like gas to wreak havoc on
                               them from within.

These instances made Rose Petal practitioners wield their hilts
while manipulating a shiny fog
                     through their enemy's skin as they
executed various katas that looked
                     like hand-to-hand combat while each tried
moving the steel dust they
                     controlled into a prime position for
                         incapacitating their opponent.
Sometimes the heat of these
close confrontations
and movements let frustration give way
to hard, direct blows with

the solid hilts,
closing another circle of progress.

EMOTIONAL ARMOUR MERCHANT

Welcome to my shop! I have protective wares if you have coin
to defend your ego, like soft loins, against being sensitive
in ways figurative or real, and that barrier is addictive,
like a permissive armour set letting opaque eye holes
fill mind bowls with nothing but the faults of others;
a cloak to help you hide under covers, only useful
for a moment of fleeting hope before a blade
cuts through thin-made material around you
if you fear blue moods more than sudden death's factitude.

I'm glad you're still alive,
I can get you a suit boosting indifference by five if you fight
the creature
whose main attack makes you apologise
before it moves to actualise a reality
predicated on your capacity to perceive
fault first, so you heave everyone's
accountability onto your shoulders,
and guard a border by the command of flattering orders.

Forgot a purchase? It's alright, take your time,
you can still perform a pantomime to survive
if you arrive wearing these molten lava plates
that change fate by keeping you from moving
past first feelings to heights of responsible reflection,
staying forever in an elemental eruption blasting out,
a cathartic shout burning every tree away,
while most stay back to avoid your bad days.

I've got new stock; it might be a bit beyond your budget
to gather material and shove it into the shape of an altar
that'll never falter in convincing them of your intent,
a sculpted knight without a dent, not encasing your body,
but granting your shoddy faults a perfect veneer
of accomplishment to veer criticism from beyond or within
towards the garbage bin, and to absorb, when it comes to it,
the aim of guns borne by those feeling finished.

Did I already say I'm not from here?
In my land we see fear as a thing you have to appease,
with safety based on the ease of given obedience,
so our experience is one of giving in, to keep
harm in the distant deep without needing defences
blocking our delicate senses from being negatively hurt,
and the burning, curt pleas of family wanting us well
until we float above hell and below heaven,
alone in some craven forest of the raven.

You need armour? Go on, see what I offer.
I have light suits whose fur may not block a strike
but whose sharp hairs are like prods pushing you
into a view of attacking first to guard
against enemies, going hard on their ability to initiate,
moving straight to destruction before it can rise,
then your eyes see you as being impervious
to odious resentments or winds of the attritious.

I do hope to see you again;
I have few repeat customers and some that are new,
frantic to climb out of spiritual grime.

Some I never see again,
whether they've made a space that ended their chase
or they've drowned in issues with which they're crowned.
Though, if true,
I keep the second option far from my mental view.

THROUGH THE PATTERNS AND THE SOUL

Every thought is a
lightning strike for the
inhabitants of
planets throughout her
synapse nebula.

When a mind acts out
of its own volition
there are logical
patterns, if only
you see on their scale.

The universe's
overseer is
the process of all
its mechanics, its
colossal motions.

They don't see our lives
as trivial; it's
just that our flora
and their galaxies
share star DNA.

How else can we
face this blossom
but with caution
while curious,

keeping one
quality
in each eye

at the
same time?

A mineral
hung on your neck
that never spins
can anchor you

as blurred lights spiral
out to carry off
copies of yourself,
imagined by those
viewing your breakdown,

who don't look when
your disparate
elements work
in harmony,

saying that
such grace must
be a myth.

STARING DOWN THE REDUCED BLUE DRAGON AND THE MAN CLOTHED IN MOONS

Windstorms coming through my cracked mirror
    howl and wail in harmonies
            of an avant-garde symphony.

I reinforce the frame to perfection,
  winning awards for designs
  holding back my other half

but only someone
       sentenced to mirror construction
       understands what it's like
       staring down my reversal
       whenever his soul inflammation
              flares up,

who might as well say
Hello, Clarice,
       with an expression
       like sharpened diamonds
       clear enough to show
what dies so inner fires can feed
              and how.

He smiles in his cell

  whose walls have photoreal sketches
  of every rotten thought I've discarded.
  They come off their pages if he eats them for strength
  when pursuing good
pushes me through his natural realm,

then demon wings unfold
  from his finely tailored prison garb,
  blood froths instead of saliva in his mouth,
and instruments for orchestrating pain
  appear on his meal tray.

Those same tools
 have torn into me.
I see them on the floor by my feet
  while their cuts in my skin
    scab over with infernal magma
  urging this body to reach over,
   pick them up, and continue their saga.

I say *This body,*
because it won't be me anymore if I do,
within shades of shifting culpability,
manipulating my identity
   into fading from view

though envisioning that outcome to avoid
  brings his blighted fantasy
too close to my reality.

An opaque partition
in place of plexiglass

is out of the question.

His invisibility
simply means
   I'll sense him everywhere he could appear,
   only containing what he is
   by knowing his location
through a constant vigil of what I'm blessedly not,
       conjoined with visceral warnings
           of what I could become,
      angling my stance
           off to one side,
      without letting a reflection of myself
line up with his visage
in the soft, transparent barrier
        between our private yards.

ON THE DAY LOU REED DIED

On the day Lou Reed died
a black light bard
for the backs of banquet halls
                  fell silent
while new arrivals entered
their long, nameless nocturne
with only memories of his shadow's
shapeful guidance
showing an existence
        they might follow.

On the day Lou Reed died
I didn't realise
how I'd decided to abandon
drug connoisseurs with card decks in their hats,
delirious disco mystics
and Parkdale's soon-to-be dead
                  but I did.
There's coal a furnace burns
and coal that cascades in avalanches of smoke
through which the sun
            becomes your personal demon.

On the day Lou Reed died
I accepted how some essence of his famed hostility
                      manifested in me.
It'd already oxidised
half my internal organs beyond repair

and holding through the knee-jerk jolt
in the irritation of an honest reflection
let me look at my anger long enough to formulate
an engine I made run with its fissures

but containing the resultant radioactivity
enough to continue is key,
and Lieutenant Spock will tell you
how managing that isn't so easy.

On the day Lou Reed died
my brother poured me a shot of whiskey
and would have offered ether
if it had been the 1890s
when I started amputating half my rusted heart
that still, surprisingly,
pulled away quickly
as I plunged in the blade,
but that part had long since
        had enough of me
impeding its freedom
        to change chemically.

Keeping it meant tetanus,
cutting it off meant entering a state of unbalanced tilting,
from which many
never adjust their alignment.
And I could only hope
        that one day I might,
though I'm not sure if I have
        or if I ever will.

On the day Lou Reed died,
mall date memories melted
as I drifted
into an industrial unit's
underground gallery.

Hemingway may have had Paris's moveable feast,
but most of us carry the pop-art beauty
of local takeout
as the totems
to which we're tethered.

On the day Lou Reed died
the characters of my life's Warhol factory
started looking less
like an explosion, inevitably propelling me
over furniture conferences
or cottage remembrances,
        and more like primal fires who never made
the embers of warm memories smoulder
                in normal locations;
they looked more
like claw machine prizes
possessed by spite,
pulling down
those calling prongs to pick them up:

one was an acid-dosed monk
smashing tables
before chasing friends into the closet
with a weaponized wooden leg;

one disappeared into his house,
emerging later with a crusted brand
in the back of his hand,

astrologers sat in spider-filled apartments,

someone made themselves the canvas,
weaving ribbon through rings piercing flesh

and that's a baby step
before becoming he who
hung himself by his skin in the gallery,
        a body canvas on display,

and even the poet who cut off one thumb with a mitre saw
managed to draft his fractured state
on cardboard with crayon
then recite it to the stump onstage.

On the day Lou Reed died
I set out on a long, fitful journey
      towards who I really am,
          where what I do
     might not affect everyone I envision,
though it may impact someone,
     and in our world of gravity so greatly increased
     that could be enough
     to make a noteworthy achievement, somewhere,
     since somebody's always left behind
when everybody ascends,
   to a supposedly greater plain.

Acknowledgements

"Vainglorious Purpose!" first published as a spoken word recording in the Poets in Response to Peril video anthology by Owen Sound Poet Laureate Richard-Yves Sitoski

"You Can't Reflect Here; This is the Prayer Room" first published as "Move that Tank" in the Poets for Ukraine Anthology edited by David Brydges

"There's Wisdom in the Crimson Mural" first published in Blank Spaces Magazine (March 2023)

"The Ultraviolet Mitigator" first published in Martian Magazine

"Ethereal Ink Bleeding Through" first published in Lothlorien Poetry Journal

"In the Realm of Reanimation" first published in MONO Fiction

"Too Quiet on the Open Front" first published as "The Suspicious Patient" in Mulberry Literary Journal

"Advertising in a Conformative Marketing Environment" first published in Purely Liminal Magazine

"I Chose…Poorly" first published in Meat for Tea: The Valley Review

"Effexor Withdrawal Variations" first published in Pinhole Poetry Magazine

"The Angels of Our Synchronised Awareness" first published in the Clown House Arts Collaborative Chapbook - SPARK UP Edition

"Enter the Liquid Word" first published in Clinch Literary Magazine

"Knife Demons in the Shape of Gentlemen" first published in Sein Und Werden (Become and Becoming) Quarterly Literary Journal

"Rose Oceania" first published in the Flower-Shaped Bullet Anthology by Loud Coffee Press

"Staring Down the Reduced Blue Dragon and the Man Clothed in Moons" first published partially in the Open Skies Poetry Anthology

About the Poet

Paul Edward Costa (He/Him) is an award-winning poet, spoken word artist, and teacher. He is a former Poet Laureate for the City of Mississauga, the Director of the Outer Haven Poetry series, and a full member of the League of Canadian Poets. He won the 2019 Mississauga Arts Council's Emerging Literary Arts Award and his poetry has appeared in publications such as *Poetry Undressed Quarterly, Train: A Poetry Journal, Blank Spaces Magazine, and Brickyard Spoken Word*. His full-length poetry collection, *The Long Train of Chaos*, was released by Kung Fu Treachery Press in 2019 and his book of flash fiction, *God Damned Avalon*, was published by Mosaic Press in 2021. As a spoken word artist, Paul has featured at many poetry readings online and in-person such as The Art Bar Poetry Series, Shab-e She'r, Wild Writers, The Oh!Sound Reading Series, the Oakville Literary Cafe, Port Veritas Poetry, Laureate City by VerseFest in Ottawa, and Tongues of Fire by the Victoria Poetry Project. He was a team member with Sauga Poetry and has hosted or co-hosted past poetry or open mic series like the YTGA Open Mic at Studio.89, the Art Bar Poetry Series, and Verses Out Loud. Follow him on Twitter, YouTube, Instagram, and Facebook.

Facebook: https://m.facebook.com/PaulEdwardCosta/
YouTube: https://www.youtube.com/PaulEdwardCosta
Instagram: https://www.instagram.com/paul.edward.costa/
Twitter: @paul_e_costa

www.ingramcontent.com/pod-product-compliance
Lightning Source LLC
Chambersburg PA
CBHW070949180426
43194CB00041B/1901